WRITE IT
A Guide for Research

Elizabeth Bankhead
Carole Martinez
Janet Nichols
Ruth Anne Windmiller

Ann Richards
Consultant

LIBRARIES UNLIMITED, INC.

Englewood, Colorado
1988

LIBRARIES UNLIMITED, INC.
P.O. Box 6633
Englewood, CO 80155-6633

_____

Library of Congress Cataloging-in-Publication Data

Write it.

    1. Report writing. 2. Research. I. Bankhead,
Elizabeth.
[LB1047.3.W75   1988]   808'.02   88-13729
ISBN 0-87287-676-4 single copy
ISBN 0-87287-665-9 set of 10

TABLE OF CONTENTS

ACKNOWLEDGMENTS

When we wrote this guide, we wanted to create a writing guide to meet the present and future needs of Cherry Creek High School students and teachers in Denver, Colorado. Many people have contributed to its completion. Maxine Brandt Norberg recognized the need for a high school writing guide in the 1960s and played an important role in the first editions of *Write It*. The English and Social Studies departments have been helpful with ideas about form and format: especially Pat Streeter for her editorial support, Paulette Wasserstein for her contribution to the thesis statement page, Susan Roberts for her suggestions on documentation, and Janet Sammons for her help with bibliography cards.

We also thank the library support staff, including parent volunteers, who gave us the time to undertake this project and Henry Cotton, our principal, for his personal commitment to reading, his professional confidence and support, and his commitment to excellence, which have made a strong library program possible. Finally, we thank the students of Cherry Creek High School for insisting upon excellence, for asking the hard questions, and for continuing to challenge us to evaluate our program.

Betty Bankhead/Program Coordinator
Carole Martinez/Computer Coordinator
Janet Nichols/Resources Coordinator
Ruth Anne Windmiller/Instructional Coordinator
Ann Richards/Thinking Skills Consultant

In composing this guide, we used the following publications as sources of information and standards of form:

Campbell, William Giles, Stephen Vaughan Ballow, and Carol Slade. *Form and Style: Theses, Reports, Term Papers*. 6th edition. Boston: Houghton Mifflin, 1982.

Gibaldi, Joseph, and Walter S. Achtert. *MLA Handbook for Writers of Research Papers*. 2nd edition. New York: The Modern Language Association of America, 1984.

Markman, Roberta H., Peter F. Markman, and Marie L. Waddell. *10 Steps in Writing the Research Paper*. 3rd edition. Woodbury, New York: Barron's Educational Series, Inc., 1982.

Roth, Audrey J. *The Research Paper: Form and Content*. Belmont, Calif.: Wadsworth Publishing Company, Inc., 1978.

Turabian, Kate L. *Manual for Writers of Term Papers, Theses & Dissertations*. 5th edition. Chicago: University of Chicago Press, 1987.

TO STUDENTS USING
WRITE IT

Very few good high school courses are taught solely from textbooks or totally within a classroom. Teachers know you will need to know much more after high school than facts learned from texts. For that reason, your teachers will assign a variety of readings, reports, debates, and research papers, and most of the information you will need for those assignments will be in your library.

Art teachers want you to compare the works of different artists so you can begin to decide what you like. History teachers want you to read and compare many accounts of one historical event so you can learn to evaluate the different accounts of political events reported in the news every day. Science teachers want you to find and read journal articles about recent scientific developments so you can learn to use technical information to make important personal lifestyle decisions. Business teachers want you to compare products in consumer magazines so you can learn to find information to help you make difficult purchases. English teachers want you to write about the books you read and use word processing technology to make revisions so you can learn to communicate effectively in the writing your job will demand.

The information and technology you need, and the people with the expertise to teach you to use both, can be found in your school Library Media Center. *Write It* is designed to help you find information in the library and to learn to present your findings in a way that will also be accepted in other classes and later in business or professional life. The two people who will show you how to use this guide are your teacher and your Library Media Specialist. Your teacher will make an assignment after consulting with the Library Media Specialist about the information available and the techniques you will need to find it. Then your teacher and Library Media Specialist will teach you the best way to find, evaluate, and report your information, using *Write It*.

Write It is divided into three parts:

- The first part gives you ways to locate information easily. Also remember, your Library Media Specialist is the expert on what your library has, so you will want to ask for guidance with your search strategy.

- The second part of *Write It* shows you how to present and document your information as a formal research paper. This section includes examples of note cards, bibliography cards, footnotes, and also hints to help you write a better paper.

- The third part of *Write It* is the appendix which includes directions for writing an abstract of a journal article, science and social science documentation, plus how to type or word process and print a completed paper.

Write It should help you find information for most of your assignments. However, remember that once you move into advanced classes or advanced research, your Library Media Specialist can give you information on ways to find additional resources in the public and academic libraries in your area.

USING THE LIBRARY

FINDING INFORMATION IN THE LIBRARY

General Reference and Background Reading

A good place to begin your search for information is the general reference sources because they will help you with dates, principal people, and background information, as well as with narrowing your subject. These general references, however, do not have the detailed information needed for most high school research. Some good sources of general information are

TEXTBOOKS
ENCYCLOPEDIAS
ALMANACS
DICTIONARIES

Detailed Information

The next place to go to find out what information is available on your topic is the card catalog. Books in the card catalog are listed under three types of cards: subject, author, and title cards. In addition to the card catalog, many larger libraries have computerized their collections. The computer generally will ask you to input the subject, author, or title, and display the information in a format that is standard for that library. (To find more about how to find lists of subjects, see Appendix A: Finding Alternative Subject Headings.)

SUBJECT CARD

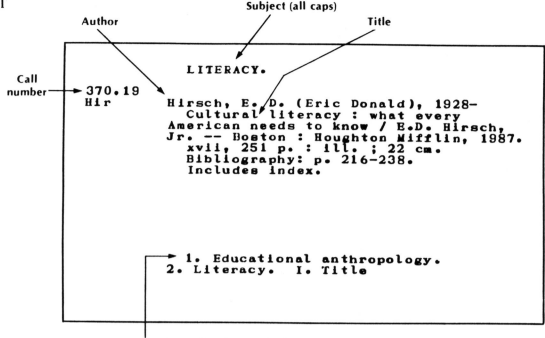

Tracings—listed near the bottom of the card and give other general subjects under which a book is listed.

COMPUTER SUBJECT SEARCH

```
-------------------------------------------------------------
AUTHOR(s):      Hirsch, E. D. (Eric Donald), 1928-
TITLE(s):       Cultural literacy : what every American needs to know /
                   E.D. Hirsch, Jr. ; with an appendix, What literate
                   Americans know [by] E.D. Hirsch, Jr., Joseph Kett,
                   James Trefil.

                Boston : Houghton Mifflin, 1987.
                xvii, 251 p. :  ill. ; 22cm.
                Includes index.
                Bibliography: p. 216-238
                JD  NORLIN [c.1]

OTHER ENTRIES:  Literacy  United States.
                Educational anthropology  United States.
                Culture.
                Kett, Joseph F.
                Trefil, James S.,  1938-

CALL #: LC149  .H57 1987                    LOCN:  NORLIN
STATUS: On Reserve --
-------------------------------------------------------------
<RETURN> to continue, <Q>UIT for a new search, or <R> to REPEAT this
display
```

AUTHOR CARD

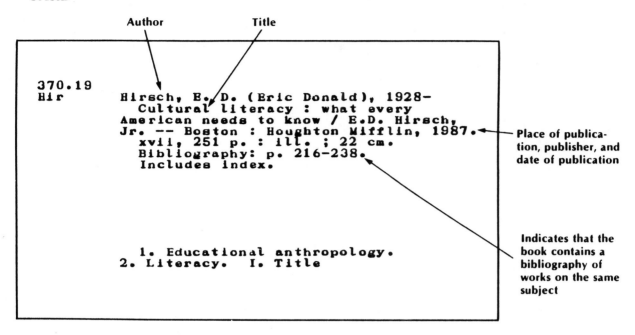

Author   Title

370.19
Hir

Hirsch, E. D. (Eric Donald), 1928–
   Cultural literacy : what every
American needs to know / E.D. Hirsch,
Jr. –– Boston : Houghton Mifflin, 1987.
  xvii, 251 p. : ill. ; 22 cm.
  Bibliography: p. 216-238.
  Includes index.

   1. Educational anthropology.
2. Literacy. I. Title

Place of publication, publisher, and date of publication

Indicates that the book contains a bibliography of works on the same subject

TITLE CARD

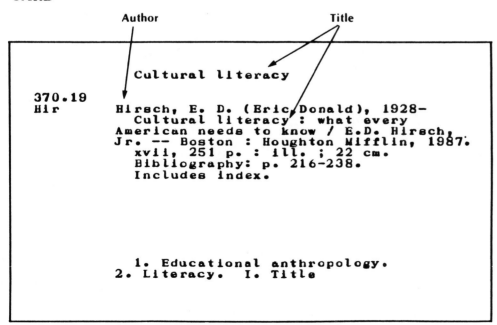

Author   Title

   Cultural literacy

370.19
Hir

Hirsch, E. D. (Eric Donald), 1928–
   Cultural literacy : what every
American needs to know / E.D. Hirsch,
Jr. –– Boston : Houghton Mifflin, 1987.
  xvii, 251 p. : ill. ; 22 cm.
  Bibliography: p. 216-238.
  Includes index.

   1. Educational anthropology.
2. Literacy. I. Title

LOCATING CURRENT INFORMATION

1. To find current magazine articles, see

READERS' GUIDE. Bimonthly index to 179 popular magazines and journals by subject and author of each article. Book reviews can be found at the end of each volume.

MAGAZINE INDEX. Microfilm index to over 400 journals and popular magazines by author and subject.

READERS' GUIDE		MAGAZINE INDEX
Sample Entry		Sample Entry

Astronomy ——————————————— Subject ——— **ASTRONOMY**

    See also

    Artificial satellites – Astronomical use   see also

    Asteroids   Aeronomics in Astronomy

    Black holes (Astronomy)   Astronomy

    Comets   Other places   Galaxies – Evolution

    Communications satellites – Astronomical use   to look in   Geodesy

    Computers - Astronomical use   the index   Milkyway

       Satellites

       Seasons

    Charts, diagrams, etc.

    See also

    Stars – Atlases ——————————— Title of article

Astronomy [laser disk] D. H. Smith. *Sky Telesc* 72:593 +   -ACHIEVEMENTS AND AWARDS

D '86   Appointments and awards. Sky and Telescope

New northern sky survey [Palomar Sky Survey] *Sci News*   Volume   v72-July'86 31(1)   34K4963

130:295 N 8 '86   number   Krupp honored with AIP science writing

     award for second time. il Physics Today

     v38-Dec'85 p.72(2)

    Terminology   Date of

The spelling lesson. D. Lago. il *Astronomy* 14:32 + D   magazine

'86   -AUSTRALIA

     Excerpts from an Australian Journal by

     Title of   Dennis Di Cicco (astrophotography) il

    Australia   magazine   Sky and Telescope

Excerpts from an Australian journal. D. Di Cicco. il *Sky*   v72-Oct'86 p.344(4)   35L5111

Telesc 72:344-7 O '86   Author

     -CHARTS, DIAGRAMS, ETC.

    France   Celestial Events. (October 1983) (column) by

The dawn of balloon astronomy [work of A. de la Baume-   Thomas d. Nicholson il Natural History

Pluvinel on solar spectrum] D. H. DeVorkin. il por *Sky*   v92-Oct'83 p.96(2)

Telesc 72:579-81 D '86

     Page

     number

2. To find newspaper articles, see

NEWSBANK. Microfiche copies of full text of selected articles from over 450 U.S. newspapers arranged annually by subject.

NEW YORK TIMES CURRENT EVENTS EDITION. Microfiche copies of news articles from the New York Times with brief summaries, names, and dates arranged annually by subject.

NEW YORK TIMES CRITICAL ISSUES. Microfiche copies of news articles, editorials, and analyses from the New York Times. Contains the 12 most frequently researched topics in high school compiled annually.

EDITORIALS ON FILE. Twice-monthly reprints of newspaper editorials on timely issues from U.S. and Canadian newspapers.

3. To find reprints of both magazine and newspaper articles, see

OPPOSING VIEWPOINTS SOURCES. Primary and secondary source reprints reflecting opposing points of view on controversial topics.

SIRS (Social Issues Resources Series). Reprints of articles covering current social and scientific issues.

4. To find facts and statistics, see

FACTS ON FILE. A weekly world news digest of names, dates, statistics, and events with a yearly cumulative index.

ALMANACS. Annual listing of facts, statistics, population distribution, awards, etc.

5. To find in-depth reports and documents, see

EDITORIAL RESEARCH REPORTS. Weekly in-depth studies of a current issue of national significance with background statistics and predictions for the future. Reports are bound semi-annually with an index to all of the volumes.

CONGRESSIONAL QUARTERLY WEEKLY REPORTS. Weekly update on foreign policy, politics, Supreme Court cases, and congressional legislation. Weekly reports are located in semi-annual binders with complete index.

WRITING THE RESEARCH PAPER

WHAT IS A RESEARCH PAPER?

Research means to "seek out again," and its purpose is to bring together old and new information and documented recent opinions that have not been previously brought together: in writing the paper you use this information as evidence in support of a thesis. The research paper involves your ability to gather information, examine it, think about it, organize it, and write about it.

Although teachers' assignments vary, the research paper (sometimes called the term paper, research report, investigative assignment) usually involves all of the following:

1. careful research of already existing ideas, facts, and expert opinions on a specific topic

2. a thesis statement proven with facts, ideas, and expert opinions

3. a formal presentation of your research and thesis

HOW IS A RESEARCH PAPER DIFFERENT FROM A REPORT?

A research assignment is more than a report. You have written reports in elementary school and middle school or junior high school. You will continue to write reports in some courses in high school and probably as part of any job. What makes research differ from reporting information and facts is that you must

1. analyze the information you find

2. select those portions that support your opinion or thesis

3. convince your reader your conclusions are correct

4. and finally, show your reader the sources of the information in a bibliography of sources, and acknowledge the writers who had those ideas by giving them credit in notes

A research assignment should give you experience not only with locating information but also with evaluating, analyzing, and reacting to that information.

PLAGIARISM

Plagiarism is copying or accepting another person's work without acknowledging it, whether the work is published or unpublished, professional or amateur. If you use another's words, ideas, opinions, study, and/or facts, you must document them in the form of a footnote or endnote. Whenever you are gathering information for the research paper, be sure to make clear on your notecard whose material it is. Paraphrasing another's words is not enough to avoid plagiarism. Any material (ideas or words) taken from another person must be documented.

Remember that it does not matter whether stealing another's words, ideas, or opinions was intentional. If you use even a small number of another's words, you are committing plagiarism. Thus, most teachers require accurate notes and documentation.

RESEARCH PAPER PROCESS CHECKLIST

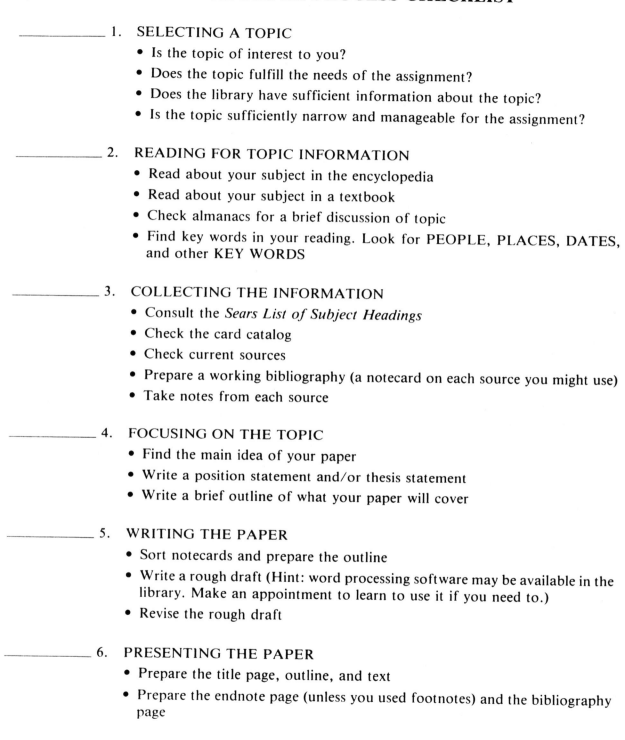

_____ 1. SELECTING A TOPIC
- Is the topic of interest to you?
- Does the topic fulfill the needs of the assignment?
- Does the library have sufficient information about the topic?
- Is the topic sufficiently narrow and manageable for the assignment?

_____ 2. READING FOR TOPIC INFORMATION
- Read about your subject in the encyclopedia
- Read about your subject in a textbook
- Check almanacs for a brief discussion of topic
- Find key words in your reading. Look for PEOPLE, PLACES, DATES, and other KEY WORDS

_____ 3. COLLECTING THE INFORMATION
- Consult the *Sears List of Subject Headings*
- Check the card catalog
- Check current sources
- Prepare a working bibliography (a notecard on each source you might use)
- Take notes from each source

_____ 4. FOCUSING ON THE TOPIC
- Find the main idea of your paper
- Write a position statement and/or thesis statement
- Write a brief outline of what your paper will cover

_____ 5. WRITING THE PAPER
- Sort notecards and prepare the outline
- Write a rough draft (Hint: word processing software may be available in the library. Make an appointment to learn to use it if you need to.)
- Revise the rough draft

_____ 6. PRESENTING THE PAPER
- Prepare the title page, outline, and text
- Prepare the endnote page (unless you used footnotes) and the bibliography page

HINT: Remember that you can enhance your project with charts, diagrams, illustrations, overhead transparencies, computer graphics, handouts, etc. Computer and A-V production equipment, materials, and instruction on their use are available in your library.

DEVELOPING A THESIS STATEMENT

The following examples show how to develop a thesis statement from a broad, general idea. Each step shows a further narrowing of the topic in order to ultimately arrive at a legitimate thesis statement.

Broad ──► Narrow

Mark Twain ──────────► *Huckleberry Finn* ──────────► Biographical significance of the ending

THESIS: HUCK'S DEPARTURE AT THE END OF THE NOVEL REFLECTS TWAIN'S OWN DISSATISFACTION WITH CIVILIZATION.

Broad ──► Narrow

Public Schools ──────────► Length of school year ──────────► Positive effect of long school year

THESIS: AN EXTENDED SCHOOL YEAR WOULD HAVE A POSITIVE EFFECT ON LEARNING, STUDENT ATTITUDES TOWARD SCHOOL, AND THE RETENTION OF SKILLS FROM YEAR TO YEAR.

WHAT A THESIS STATEMENT SHOULD NOT BE:

1. A topic or subject by itself cannot serve as a thesis statement. That information tells what the paper is about, but not what you and your research has to say about the manner.

2. A question cannot serve as a thesis statement because it is not a statement. A question merely says that an answer will follow.

3. A general statement that lacks a detailed point of view cannot serve as a thesis statement. A general statement may give the reader background information but does not reflect your point of view.

WHAT A THESIS STATEMENT SHOULD BE:

1. A complete sentence summarizing the point of view in your paper.

2. A specific declaration of your main idea.

3. A statement reflecting your position.

EXAMPLES:

THESIS: Although Henry Ford has been considered an American hero, he was an egotistical business tycoon.

THESIS: Atwood's use of the twin imagery in *Surfacing* is an artistic attempt to show the dual nature of the female, a nature consisting of both the mystic and the practical.

HINT: You write a thesis statement early to focus your attention — not your reader's. Therefore, as you do your research you may wish to modify your position or radically change it. That's O.K., but you need to discuss a major change with your teacher.

PREPARING BIBLIOGRAPHY CARDS

Each source you use to write your paper must have its own bibliography card. Information is put on cards so that you may shuffle the cards into alphabetical order when preparing the final bibliography page and so that you may add and discard cards when necessary. In general, bibliography cards contain the following:

Books	Articles

(Find information on the title page and the back of the title page.)

(Find information in the periodicals index, the article itself, or the contents page of the magazine.)

Books

Author(s) or editor(s), last
   name first

Title of the book

Edition information
   (1st ed., 2nd ed., Rev. ed., etc.)

City location of publisher
   (use the first city listed)

Name of publisher

Date of publication
   (use the most recent date listed)

Volumes (if more than one)

Articles

Author(s), last name first

Title of the article

Title of publication or magazine

Volume number

Date of publication

Page numbers

BOOK:

Author → Mandell, Richard. Sport: A Cultural History. New York: Columbia University Press, 1984.

Title (titles of books are underlined)
Place of publication
Publisher
Date of publication

MORE BIBLIOGRAPHY CARD SAMPLES

MAGAZINE:

Author ——→

Volume number ——→

Severy, Merle. "The World of Suleyman the Magnificent." National Geographic, 172 (November 1987), pp. 552-601.

←—— Title of article (in quotation marks)

←—— Name of magazine (underlined)

←—— Pages

←—— Date of article

SIRS:

Author ——→

Date of article ——→

SIRS title (underlined) ——→

SIRS article number ——→

Cannon, Angie. "Steroids: Scary Student Body Fad." Miami Herald, December 21, 1986 (Reprinted in Social Issues Resources Series, Youth, 3, Article No. 20).

←—— Title of article (in quotation marks)

←—— Title of magazine

←—— Volume of SIRS

←—— Name of SIRS index

REFERENCE BOOK:

Author of article ——→

Title of article (in quotation marks) ——→

Publisher ——→

Locker, Frances Carol, ed. "Hemingway, Ernest, 1899-1961." Contemporary Authors. Vols. 77-80. Detroit: Gale Research Co., 1979.

←—— Title of book (underlined)

←—— Place of publication

←—— Date of publication

HOW TO PREPARE NOTE CARDS

EACH NOTE CARD SHOULD CONTAIN:

only one idea
a specific topic label
the author of the work (if no author, use title)
a note (one of the three types)
the page number(s)

WHAT TO NOTE:

any information that supports the thesis
facts
statistics
definitions
opinions from authorities on the subject

Use a DIRECT QUOTATION note when the author has phrased something particularly well; when the words express a meaning as no other words could; or when an authority has concisely stated an opinion about your thesis.

Steps to follow:

1. Copy the quotation exactly.
2. Check to make sure you have copied all spelling and punctuation exactly.
3. Make sure that the section of the work you quote doesn't need the surrounding material to keep the same meaning.

Topic heading	Modern Sport Mandell **Author**
DIRECT QUOTATION NOTE	"Modern sports, therefore, are particular adaptions to modern economic, social, and political life...."
Page number	p. 3

Use a PARAPHRASE NOTE most of the time. Paraphrasing is putting another's ideas into your words.

Steps to follow:

1. Ask yourself the author's purpose and/or main idea.
2. Put the idea into *your own words*.
3. Read what you have written and make sure that it reflects the author's idea.

Topic heading →	Modern Sport Mandell ← **Author**
PARAPHRASE NOTE	America does not have a Cabinet post for sports like some modern countries; or any definitive policy. Private sources are primary supporters for national and international competitions.
Page number →	p. 275

Use a SUMMARY NOTE to record in your own words the essence of a passage without examples and explanations. Usually summary notes are for less important or repetitive information.

Steps to follow:

1. Ask yourself the author's purpose and/or main idea.
2. Write that idea in a few words.

Topic heading →	Modern sport Mandell ← **Author**
SUMMARY NOTE	Modern sport must have — urban population literate people good transportation wage earners democratic ideology
Page number →	p. 275

HINT: 1. Make sure you know what is quoted and what is paraphrased.
        2. Make sure a page number is on each card before you leave the library.

PREPARING THE OUTLINE

Some teachers require that students do a "working" or "preliminary" outline before they begin to take notes. This type of outline helps to focus the research: in other words, it tells you what information you will need to find. Even if your teacher does not require a working outline, you may wish to develop one. After you have a thesis statement and have read at least two general articles, ask yourself the following two questions:

1. What will I have to discuss in order to prove my topic? (Think in terms of places, names, issues, events)

2. What keywords appeared in my general reading that may help me prove my thesis statement?

Then jot these ideas down, using the format given below. Once you have your notes completed, you need to develop an outline. This outline will be the basis of your organization: it will tell you how to form paragraphs and how to support your topic sentence, and how to arrange the material in your paper.

Steps to Developing an Outline

1. Sort your note cards by topic headings.

2. Organize these topics so that there is a logical development.

3. Create subtopics that are logical divisions of the main topic. (Each A must have a B and each 1 must have a 2 because one cannot logically divide something into only 1 part.)

4. Make sure that the wording of each line is consistent in form and phrasing. Make sure the form meets the teacher's requirements (phrases or sentences).

No matter what kind of outline your teacher requires, basic outline form is as follows:

    I.
        A.
        B.
            1.
            2.
                a.
                b.

    II.
        A.
            1.
            2.
        B.

WRITING THE ROUGH DRAFT

If you have done a good job writing your note cards and preparing an outline, then writing the paper itself will be fairly easy. Some ideas for writing the rough draft are as follows:

- put your note cards in order and use them as a guide
- keep your outline in front of you to guide your writing
- keep your thesis right in front of you and refer to it often — remember it is the point you are trying to make
- be sure to footnote quotations
- make sure that each paragraph is related to the thesis and contains only one idea, which is expressed by a topic sentence and supported by the other sentences

The research paper generally requires the following:

INTRODUCTION
- a few sentences that help the reader understand the topic and the author's position
- the thesis statement

BODY
- multiple paragraphs containing the main ideas supporting the thesis
- specific details (facts, authorities' views, studies) that prove main ideas

CONCLUSION
- summarizes the paper's stand
- discusses the significance of the topic and/or the findings

For documentation in the research paper, the following must be acknowledged with either a footnote or an endnote:

- all direct quotations
- any idea that is not your own
- facts not generally known (Information that can be found in most general articles is not documented. Shakespeare's date of death is not documented.)
- unusual or distinctive ideas or arguments or theories (If someone says that Shakespeare was really a group of female writers, document it.)
- any opinion (an idea that is unsupported by evidence)

You do not need to document:
- an idea you thought of yourself and did not see anywhere else
- a fact or information that is general knowledge or can be easily verified in a number of sources

COMPILING THE BIBLIOGRAPHY

Usually the bibliography consists of an alphabetical listing of the sources you cited in your notes and additional sources you used but did not cite. For example, you would include an encyclopedia article that you read for background information.

The following section gives examples of sources cited first as notes and then as bibliographic entries. Refer to these examples as you prepare your own notes and bibliography.

NOTE AND BIBLIOGRAPHY FORMS

When first referring to a source in notes or bibliography, full documentation should be given. The following examples are shown in pairs: footnote or endnote form first, then bibliography form.

Books

One Author

[1]Richard Mandell, Sport: A Cultural History (New York: Columbia University Press, 1984), p. 4.

Mandell, Richard. Sport: A Cultural History. New York: Columbia University Press, 1984.

Two or Three Authors

[2]Carol Pearson and Katherine Pope, The Female Hero in American and British Literature (New York: R. R. Bowker Company, 1981), pp. 92-93.

Pearson, Carol, and Katherine Pope. The Female Hero in American and British Literature. New York: R. R. Bowker Company, 1981.

Four or More Authors and an Edition

[3]Richard R. Bootzin and others, Psychology Today: An Introduction, 6th ed. (New York: Random House, 1986), p. 197.

Bootzin, Richard R., and others. Psychology Today: An Introduction. 6th ed. New York: Random House, 1986.

Editor, Translator, or Compiler

[4]Otto T. Johnson, ed., <u>The 1987 Information Please Almanac</u> (Boston: Houghton Mifflin Company, 1987), p. 145.

Johnson, Otto T., ed. <u>The 1987 Information Please Almanac.</u> Boston: Houghton Mifflin Company, 1987.

Multivolume Work with Editor

[5]Frances Carol Locher, ed., "Hemingway, Ernest, 1899-1961," <u>Contemporary Authors,</u> vols. 77-80 (Detroit: Gale Research Co., 1979), p. 229.

Locher, Frances Carol, ed., "Hemingway, Ernest, 1899-1961." <u>Contemporary Authors.</u> Vols. 77-80. Detroit: Gale Research Co., 1979.

Multivolume Work or Series, Author and Editor

[6]Howard Faulkner, "Richard Wright," <u>Critical Survey of Long Fiction,</u> ed. Frank N. Magill, vol. 7 (Englewood Cliffs, N.J.: Salem Press, 1982), p. 2975.

Faulkner, Howard. "Richard Wright," <u>Critical Survey of Long Fiction.</u> Ed. Frank N. Magill. Vol. 7. Englewood Cliffs, N.J.: Salem Press, 1982.

Series with a Different Title for Each Volume

[7]T. H. Jackson and George Stade, eds., <u>The Middle Ages and the Renaissance,</u> vol. 1, <u>European Writers</u> (New York: Charles Scribner's Sons, 1983), p. 161.

Jackson, T. H., and George Stade, eds. <u>The Middle Ages and the Renaissance.</u> Vol. 1, <u>European Writers.</u> New York: Charles Scribner's Sons, 1983.

Pamphlet

[8]Eric Berg, <u>Teens and AIDS</u> (Santa Cruz, Calif.: Network Publications, 1987), p. 2.

Berg, Eric. <u>Teens and AIDS.</u> Santa Cruz, Calif.: Network Publications, 1987.

Magazines

Magazine Article with Author

[9]Merle Severy, "The World of Suleyman the Magnificent," National Geographic, 172 (November 1987), p. 563.

Severy, Merle. "The World of Suleyman the Magnificent." National Geographic, 172 (November 1987), pp. 552-601.

Magazine Article without Author

[10]"New Human Retrovirus," Science News, 132 (December 26, 1987), p. 391.

"New Human Retrovirus." Science News, 132 (December 26, 1987), p. 391.

Newspapers

Newspaper Article with Author

[11]Jack Anderson, "Nuclear Regulators Push Safety Through Loophole," Rocky Mountain News, January 5, 1984, p. 22.

Anderson, Jack. "Nuclear Regulators Push Safety Through Loophole." Rocky Mountain News, January 5, 1984.

NewsBank

[12]Peggy McCollough, "Juvenile Drug Use Prompts Test Push," Commercial Appeal, Jan. 15, 1987 (Reprinted in NewsBank, Health, 1987, fiche 3, grid G2).

McCollough, Peggy. "Juvenile Drug Use Prompts Test Push." Commercial Appeal, Jan. 15, 1987 (Reprinted in NewsBank, Health, 1987, fiche 3, grid G2).

New York Times Current Events Edition

[13]Malcom W. Browne, "World Threat of Plastic Trash Defies Technology," New York Times, Sept. 6, 1987 (Reprinted in New York Times Current Events Edition, 1987, fiche 76, grid 13A).

Browne, Malcom W. "World Threat of Plastic Trash Defies Technology." New York Times Sept. 6, 1987 (Reprinted in New York Times Current Events Edition, 1987, fiche 76, grid 13A).

Current Sources

Background Notes

[14]U.S. Department of State, "Bangladesh," Background Notes, Washington, D.C.: Government Printing Office, April 1987.

U.S. Department of State. "Bangladesh." Background Notes. Washington, D.C.: Government Printing Office, April 1987.

Culturegram

[15]"People's Republic of China," Culturegram, Provo, Utah: Brigham Young University Publication Services, 1986.

"People's Republic of China." Culturegram. Provo, Utah: Brigham Young University Publication Services, 1986.

Editorial Research Reports

[16]Harrison Donnelley, "Education Reform," Editorial Research Reports, 2 (October 23, 1987), p. 552.

Donnelley, Harrison. "Education Reform." Editorial Research Reports, 2 (October 23, 1987), pp. 550-563.

Editorials on File

[17]Editorial, Los Angeles Times, October 12, 1987 (Reprinted in Editorials on File, 18, p. 1152).

Editorial. Los Angeles Times. October 12, 1987 (Reprinted in Editorials on File, 18, p. 1152).

Facts on File

[18]"Amazon Oil Exploration Suspended," Facts on File, 47 (November 13, 1987), p. 852G1.

"Amazon Oil Exploration Suspended." Facts on File, 47 (November 13, 1987), p. 852G1.

Government Documents

[19]U.S. Bureau of the Census, <u>Statistical Abstract of the United States: 1987,</u> 107th ed. (Washington, D.C.: Government Printing Office, 1986), p. 131.

U.S. Bureau of the Census. <u>Statistical Abstract of the United States: 1987</u>. 107th ed. Washington, D.C.: Government Printing Office, 1986.

Opposing Viewpoints

[20]Jeffrey Z. Rubin and Nehemia Friedland, "Recognizing Terrorists' Concerns Could Eliminate Violence," (Reprinted in <u>Opposing Viewpoints Sources,</u> Foreign Policy, Viewpoint No. 135, p. 147).

Rubin, Zeffrey Z., and Nehemia Friedland. "Recognizing Terrorists' Concerns Could Eliminate Violence." (Reprinted in <u>Opposing Viewpoints Sources,</u> Foreign Policy, Viewpoint No. 135, pp. 145-148).

Social Issues Resources Series (SIRS)

[21]Angie Cannon, "Steroids: Scary Student Body Fad," <u>Miami Herald,</u> December 21, 1986 (Reprinted in <u>Social Issues Resources Series,</u> Youth, 3, Article No. 20).

Cannon, Angie. "Steroids: Scary Student Body Fad." <u>Miami Herald,</u> December 21, 1986 (Reprinted in <u>Social Issues Resources Series,</u> Youth, 3, Article No. 20).

Encyclopedias

Signed Encyclopedia Article

[22]C. Scott Littleton, "Mythology," <u>The World Book Encyclopedia,</u> 1987 ed., vol. 13, p. 815.

Littleton, C. Scott. "Mythology." <u>The World Book Encyclopedia,</u> 1987 ed. Vol. 13, pp. 813-830.

Unsigned Encyclopedia Article

[23]"Tibetans," <u>The Illustrated Encyclopedia of Mankind,</u> 1984 ed., vol. 14, p. 1767.

"Tibetans." <u>The Illustrated Encyclopedia of Mankind,</u> 1984 ed. Vol. 14, pp. 1765-1767.

Nonprint and Nonpublished Sources

Interview

[24]Roy Romer, Interview, Governor's Mansion, Denver, Colorado, December 2, 1987.

Romer, Roy. Interview. Governor's Mansion. Denver, Colorado, December 2, 1987.

Media (Filmstrips, Videotapes, etc.)

[25]Joan of Arc: A Portrait of a Legend, (New York: Vid America, Inc., 1985), videocassette.

Joan of Arc: A Portrait of a Legend. New York: Vid America, Inc., 1985. Videocassette.

Art/Photographs

[26]Albert Bierstadt, Rocky Pool, New Hampshire (Oil on Canvas, 18 × 24 inches), Denver Art Museum, Denver.

Bierstadt, Albert. Rocky Pool, New Hampshire (Oil on Canvas, 18 × 24 inches). Denver Art Museum, Denver.

NOTE: When you use photographs, you need to add the full data of the work in which they appear.

TV or Radio Program

[27]USA Tonight, KWGN, December 4, 1987, television broadcast.

USA Tonight. KWGN. December 4, 1987. Denver, Colorado. Television broadcast.

Unpublished Source

[28]Raylene Owen, "Using the Amaryllis Plant for a Multi-Disciplinary Investigation in Elementary/Middle School Science" (Paper presented at Smoky Hill High School for the CAST/CBTA 1988 Convention, Aurora, Colorado, March 4, 1988).

Owen, Raylene. "Using the Amaryllis Plant for a Multi-Disciplinary Investigation in Elementary/Middle School Science." Paper presented at Smoky Hill High School for the CAST/CBTA 1988 Convention. Aurora, Colorado, March 4, 1988.

Two Works by Same Author

When you use two works by the same author in a bibliography, an eight-space line is used rather than the author's name in the second entry.

BIBLIOGRAPHY EXAMPLE

Lewis, Sinclair. <u>Elmer Gantry.</u> New York: Harcourt Brace Jovanovich, Inc., 1927.

_____. <u>Main Street</u>. New York: Harcourt Brace Jovanovich, Inc., 1920.

SHORT FORMS FOR REPETITION IN NOTES

Citing the Same Source Again

After full documentation has been given for a work, use a shortened form in notes that follow. The information you include must be enough to identify the work. The author's name alone, followed by the relevant page number, is usually adequate. For example, if your first footnote is:

[1]Jack Clary, Careers in Sports (Chicago: Contemporary Books, Inc., 1982), p. 4.

and your third footnote is another reference to Clary's book, you would simply put:

[3]Clary, p. 78.

Citing More Than One Source by the Same Author

If two works by the same author have been cited or if two authors have the same last name, you need to give more information. If you note two works by the same author use the last name of the author and a shortened form of the title. Try to avoid using too many references to one source.

[2]Steinbeck, Grapes, p. 8.

[3]Steinbeck, Mice, p. 7.

Citing Sources by Authors with the Same Last Names

If you have more than one author with the same last name, use the first name to clarify.

[7]Lewis, Sinclair, p. 4.

[9]Lewis, C. S., p. 89.

Citing the Source Using Ibid.

Although in most cases it is better to use the author's last name and the page in noting a reference more than once (as shown in the forms above), some teachers may prefer that students use ibid. Ibid. is short for ibidem which is Latin for "in the same place." Ibid. can only be used if the work is cited immediately preceding it. If the page number is the same, you do not need to give it again. (Many authorities do not underline ibid. Check with your teacher.)

[2]Jack Clary, Careers in Sports (Chicago: Contemporary Books, Inc., 1982), p. 78.

[3]Ibid., p. 34.

CHECKLIST FOR REVISING YOUR RESEARCH PAPER

CONTENT and ORGANIZATION

_____ 1. Does the paper prove the thesis statement?

_____ 2. Are the generalizations supported by specific evidence?

_____ 3. Are the paragraphs centered on a clearly stated topic sentence? Are the paragraphs well developed?

_____ 4. Are quotation and paraphrases introduced and explained?

_____ 5. Are sources integrated logically and clearly?

_____ 6. Are the paragraphs related through transitions, key words, and other words?

STYLE

_____ 1. Are sentences varied in length and style?

_____ 2. Are quotations integrated into your text whenever possible? Are quotations used wisely (to describe controversial, unusual, and/or complicated ideas)?

_____ 3. Are all paraphrases and quotations documented?

_____ 4. Are the footnotes or endnotes in the correct form?

_____ 5. Is the bibliography in the correct form?

_____ 6. Does the paper contain an adequate introduction and an appropriate conclusion?

MECHANICS, USAGE, and PUNCTUATION

_____ 1. Are all sentences complete?

_____ 2. Do all subjects and verbs agree? Do all subjects and pronouns agree? (Pay special attention to *everyone, a person, someone,* etc. They are all singular so *their* cannot be used with these words.)

_____ 3. Is verb tense consistent (all past or all present)?

_____ 4. Is all spelling and typing carefully checked?

_____ 5. Is the punctuation correct?

APPENDIX A
Finding Alternative Subject Headings

One of the first and most crucial steps in using the library is knowing what words to look for in the catalog, *Readers' Guide*, and other indexes. *Sears List of Subject Headings* is a source of possible subject headings. The following is an example of an entry:

Sears List of Subject Headings

(Use for intelligent browsing)

Your topic

Astronomy 520-523

See also

Almanacs	**Outer space**
Astrology	**Planetariums**
Astrophysics	**Planets**
Bible — Astronomy	**Quasars**
Black holes (Astronomy)	**Radio astronomy**
Chronology	**Seasons**
Comets	**Solar system**
Eclipses, Lunar	**Space environment**
Eclipses, Solar	**Space sciences**
Galaxies	**Spectrum analysis**
Life on other planets	**Stars**
Meteorites	**Sun**
Meteors	**Tides**
Moon	**Zodiac**
Nautical astronomy	

All words in BOLD Print are possible subject headings

Words in light print will not be found in the card catalog or in most indexes.

xx Constellations

xx **Science; Space sciences; Stars; Universe**

(13th ed., Carmen Rovira and Caroline Reyes, eds. New York: H. W. Wilson, 1986. Used with permission of the publisher.)

HINT: The *Sears List of Subject Headings* is a good place to begin to identify key words.

APPENDIX B
Library Classification Systems

Libraries use either the Dewey Decimal System or the Library of Congress System to arrange books. Most school and public libraries use the Dewey Decimal System, which places each book into one of the following large groups:

000	General works	700	Fine arts & sports
100	Philosophy	800	Literature
200	Religion	900	History
300	Sociology		Special Sections:
400	Language		_____ Reference
500	Natural science		_____ Fiction
600	Useful arts		_____ Biography

(Add special call number designations used in your library)

Each general category is then subdivided into smaller, more specific groups. Individual books are then assigned a call number based on the small group to which they belong.

HINT: Fiction and biography (including autobiography) are filed in separate sections. Fiction is arranged alphabetically by the last name of the author. Biographies are arranged alphabetically by the last name of the person who is the subject of the biography.

Most academic libraries use the Library of Congress Classification System, which assigns a book a combination letter and number call number based on the following groups: (biography, fiction, and short stories are groups within these categories)

A	General works	M	Music
B	Philosophy, religion	N	Fine arts
C	History	P	Language and literature
D	Foreign history	Q	Science
E,F	American history	R	Medicine
G	Geography, anthropology	S	Agriculture
H	Social sciences	T	Technology
J	Political science	U	Military science
K	Law	V	Naval science
L	Education	Z	Library science, bibliography

APPENDIX C
Primary and Secondary Sources

Sometimes teachers will require the use of primary and/or secondary sources. Primary sources are the most direct kind of information: the literature, the work, letters, and so on as originally written. Secondary sources are critical and historical accounts written about these materials.

PRIMARY SOURCES

		SECONDARY SOURCES
experiments	court decisions	encyclopedias
observations	company records	textbooks
interviews	memoirs, autobiographies	reports
questionnaires	diaries	biographies
surveys	manuscripts	magazines
samplings	letters	newspapers
documents	poems	books
treaties		

EXAMPLES:

Primary Source: The original text of the Mayflower Compact as written in 1620 can be found in *Documents of American History*.

Secondary Source: An article about the lasting significance of the Mayflower Compact can be found in the *Dictionary of American History* and several other reference books.

Primary Source: The original text of the Magna Carta can be found in *Great Documents of the World: Milestones of Human Thought*.

Secondary Source: A short description of the Magna Carta can be found in *Macmillan's Concise Dictionary of World History*.

APPENDIX D
Alternate Form for
Social Science Documentation

If you write a paper for a course in the social sciences, you may be required to use a different format to cite your sources: acknowledged (documented) within the text of the paper rather than in the footnotes or endnotes. The list of references (bibliography) at the end of the paper is titled "References Cited."

EXAMPLES

Documentation within Text

If the author's name is included as part of the text, then cite only the date of the work and page number in parentheses at the end of the sentence.

> Fossey states that "poaching is only one of many pressures ... that have brought the mountain gorilla to the edge of extinction" (1981a:501).

If the author's name is not included as part of the text, then include the last name in the parentential references.

> Fossey waged a private war against human predators whom she viewed as wanton murders (Kevles 1976:74).

If the same author has written two or more works in the same year, each work is given a letter, as shown below.

> (Fossey 1981a:502)

> (Fossey 1981b:509)

List of Sources

REFERENCES CITED

Fossey, Dian. 1981a. The Imperiled Mountain Gorilla. <u>National Geographic</u> 159:501-523.

Fossey, Dian. 1981b. Death of Marachessa. <u>National Geographic</u> 159:508-511.

Kevles, Bettyann. <u>Watching the Wild Apes: The Primate Studies of Goodall, Fossey, and Galdikas.</u> New York: E. P. Dutton.

APPENDIX E
Alternate Forms for
Natural Science Documentation

When you write a paper for a science class, you may be asked to use a different format to cite your sources. Rather than using footnotes, acknowledge the sources within the text of your paper. You may do this by following the author/date format or the author/number format, depending upon the course requirement. The list of sources used (bibliography) follows the text of the paper and is titled "References Cited," "References," or another appropriate heading.

AUTHOR/DATE FORMAT

Documentation within Text

When the author's name is included as part of the text, cite only the date of the work in parentheses directly following the author's name.

> Rogoff and Rawlins (1987) state that "The existing U.S. food chain could collapse as a result of one autumn without a harvest."

When the author's name is not included as part of the text, then cite the author's name and the date of the work at the end of the sentence.

> The improving rate of human heart transplants is due primarily to gains made in medical knowledge (Berger 1987).

When the same author has written two or more works in the same year, each work is given a letter, as shown below.

> (Raloff 1986a)
>
> (Raloff 1986b)

List of Sources

REFERENCES CITED

Berger, Melvin. 1987. The Artificial Heart. New York: Franklin Watts, p. 36.

Raloff, J. 1986a. Ozone depletion's new environmental threat. Science News 130:362-363.

Raloff, J. 1986b. Low-cost way to help keep radon out. Science News 130:201.

Rogoff, Martin H., and Stephen L. Rawlins. 1987. Food security: A technological alternative. Bioscience. 37:800-807.

AUTHOR/NUMBER FORMAT

Documentation within Text

When a work is cited, include in parentheses at the point of citation the number which corresponds with the numbered citation in the bibliography. The references cited may be listed and numbered in alphabetical order or listed and numbered in the order in which they appear within the text of the paper as shown below.

> Every year in the United States over 15 million metric tons of nitrogen oxides and almost 30 million metric tons of sulfur dioxide pour into the atmosphere (1). In urban areas where concentrations of nitrogen oxides are high and organic chemicals found in gasoline are present, ozone concentrations may rise to levels harmful to health (2). Sulfur dioxide may oxidize in cloud and fog water droplets to form sulfate which is a key component of acid rain (3).

REFERENCES

1. Gay, Kathlyn. 1983. Acid Rain. New York: Franklin Watts, p. 7.

2. Abelson, Philip H. 1987. Ozone and acid rain. Science. 238:141.

3. From sulfur dioxide to sulfuric acid. Science News. 132:158.

APPENDIX F
Writing an Abstract

An abstract is a condensed statement of the most important ideas in a paper or report. The word is derived from the Latin *abstractus* to draw from or separate). The abstract may vary in length from a single sentence to several paragraphs, depending on its purpose and the nature and length of the original paper. The average length will run from 1 to 3 percent of the original or from 50 to 150 words for a 5,000-word paper.

READ THE ARTICLE

Read the report straight through to get an overview of the whole and to determine the author's main purpose.

NOTE THE MAIN FACTS

Identify the main sections and the key sentences of the original. If the article is well written, with proper transitions, this step will be easy.

WRITE THE ABSTRACT

State all the main points in complete sentences. Begin with a statement of the central idea. Then summarize all important points. Use suitable transitional words and phrases to make the finished abstract read like a connected and unified whole.

SUPPLY BIBLIOGRAPHICAL INFORMATION

At the beginning of the abstract, supply the name of the author of the article, its title, the publisher, the date and place of publication, and all necessary information for a complete bibliographic entry.

SAMPLE ABSTRACTS

Fossey, Dian. 1981. The Imperiled Mountain Gorilla. National Geographic 159:501-523.
The mountain gorilla is at the edge of extinction. Poaching, human encroachment, land clearing, illicit collecting, and tourist presence are cited as reasons for the decline of the gorilla population. Miss Fossey discusses her methods of observing gorilla behavior by mimicking their behavior in order to gain the gorilla's confidence. Fossey recounts both comic and tragic incidents experienced in her years of gorilla research. Her research centers on an effort to maintain the present gorilla population and prevent further group disintegration.

Abelson, Philip H. 1987. Ozone and acid rain. Science. 238:141.
There are no quick solutions to the problem of acid rain. When sulfur dioxide and nitrogen oxides are oxidized they are converted into more toxic and acidic substances. This can cause a rise in ozone levels harmful to health, particularly in urban areas where there are high concentrations of nitrogen oxides from vehicle emissions. A program to reduce vehicle emission of nitrous oxides is necessary and may include the use of methanol as a fuel.

APPENDIX G
Typing or Word Processing the Paper

1. Use white 8½"× 11" paper and type only on one side.

2. Set the following margins: top—one inch, bottom—one inch, sides—one inch each. Double space the text and indent the first word of the paragraph five spaces.

3. When quoting more than four typed lines, single space, and indent five spaces from *each* side. Use no quotation marks. (See quotation at top of page 39.)

TITLE PAGE

4. The title page (see example on page 38) should include only the paper's title, not in quotation marks or underlined, student's name, course name, teacher's name and date.

5. The title of the paper should use normal capitalization rules. The first word and other important words are capitalized.

DOCUMENTATION

6. Use either footnotes *or* endnotes (check with your teacher). See pages 39 and 40 and the forms shown on pages 18-24.

7. At the end of a sentence that requires documentation, put a number raised one-half space. For example, Without a doubt this recession caused "the greatest internal strife since the Civil War."[3] Always put the number at the end of a sentence—even if part of the words are your own. Some computer printers will not print superscript. Check with your teacher for an acceptable alternative. You might use (3) instead of [3].

8. Notes are numbered consecutively throughout the paper.

9. If you use endnotes, you need to create an endnote page. Label the page either "Notes" or "Endnotes." This page is placed after the text and before the bibliography page. See the example on page 40.

10. Indent each note five spaces and follow the form for the specific type of source on pages 18-24.

11. Single space within notes. Double space between notes.

12. If you are required to use footnotes, type a one-half-inch line a double space below the last line of the text, and place the first note a double space below the line. Remember that you need to keep the one-inch bottom margin. (If it is a partial page, type the one-half-inch line at the appropriate location so that the notes end at the bottom margin one inch from the bottom of the page.)

13. The last page should be the page labeled "Bibliography" and should follow the forms given on pages 18-24. Single space within works. Double space between works. See the example on page 40.

SAMPLE TITLE PAGE

Center all information

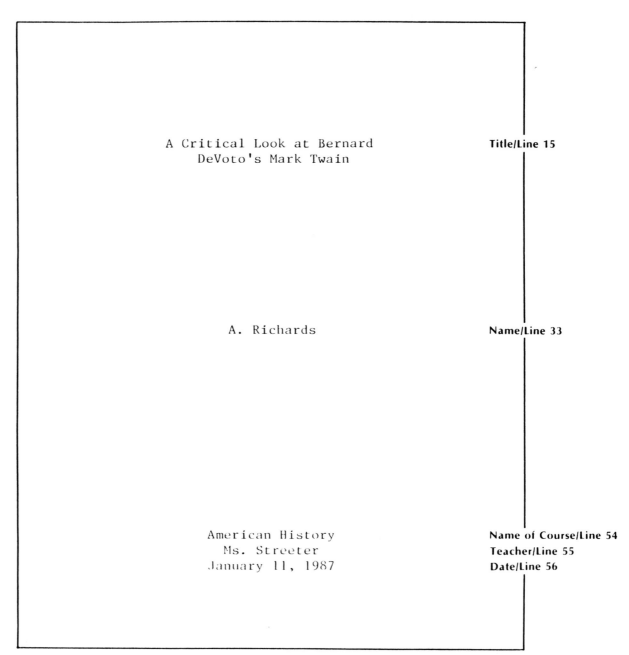

A Critical Look at Bernard   **Title/Line 15**
DeVoto's Mark Twain

A. Richards   **Name/Line 33**

American History   **Name of Course/Line 54**
Ms. Streeter   **Teacher/Line 55**
January 11, 1987   **Date/Line 56**

SAMPLE PAGE WITH FOOTNOTES

Long quotations are single spaced and indented.

Footnote numbers are always at end of sentence.

When possible work quotations into your text.

Use either endnotes or footnotes

DeVoto's love of the West cannot be ignored because it reveals his romantic view:

> The steam boat age perfectly expressed America. Even the debris through which it passed was vital and eloquent--the dens at Helena and Natchez and all the waterside slums; the shanty boats with their drifting loafers; the boats of medicine shows, daguerreotypers, thugs, whoremasters.[3]

It is doubtful that many Westerners found the thugs on the river "vital" or even "eloquent." But DeVoto's West is not all romantic whitewash; he reveals its seamy side and most of his writing is based on fact.

Throughout the book it is apparent the sources DeVoto used are impeccable. First of all, he saw the Western frontier as a mixture of ideas, cultures, and people. He saw distinctions his Eastern contemporaries did not even bother to search for.[4] One distinction that is of particular interest is the difference between a squatter and a frontier man. DeVoto discusses the West with accuracy, dealing with the folk art with special skill. One of Brook's contentions is that the West had no folk art. DeVoto scoffs at this idea. He pictures the Negro minstrel, the cockfight, the folk humorists.

To understand the knowledge of the American frontier it is necessary to look at the author himself. His interests were varied, but as his biographer points out his main interest was always history "even when the history was disguised in fiction or in social criticism."[5]

---

[3]DeVoto, p. 106.

[4]Garrett Mattingly, _Bernard DeVoto: A Preliminary Appraisal_ (Boston: Little, Brown, and Co., 1932), pp. 25-26.

[5]Orlan Sawey, _Bernard DeVoto_ (New York: Twayne Publishers, 1969), p. 73.

Footnote 3 means that DeVoto's work must have been cited in footnote 1 or 2 on a previous page.

Endnote Changes in the 4th Edition MLA Handbook
Sample Page of Endnotes

Notes

[1] VanWyck Brooks, <u>The Ordeal of Mark Twain</u> (London: William Hienemann, 1992) 25.

[2] Bernard DeVoto, <u>Mark Twain's America</u> (Cambridge: Riverside P, 1932) 320.

[3] DeVoto, 106.

[4] Garrett Mattingly, <u>Bernard DeVoto: A Preliminary Appraisal</u> (Boston: Little, Brown & Co., 1932) 25-26.

[5] DeVoto, 41, 45-51.

[6] Orlan Sawey, <u>Bernard DeVoto</u> (New York: Twayne, 1969) 73.

[7] DeVoto, 69.

[8] DeVoto, 64-74.

[9] Sawey, 57.

[10] Justin Kaplan, <u>Mr. Clemens and Mark Twain</u>, (New York: Simon and Schuster, (1966) 18.

[11] DeVoto, 240.

[12] Kaplan, 9.

[13] Lewis, Leary, ed., <u>A Casebook on Mark Twain's Wound</u> (New York: Thomas Y. Crowell Co., 1962) 158.

[14] Henry Seidel Canby, "Mark Twain Himself," <u>Saturday Review of Literature</u> 9 (1932): 201-202.

[15] Sinclair Lewis, "Fools, Liars, and Mr. DeVoto," <u>Saturday Review of Literature</u> 27 (1944): 230.

[16] Floyd Dell, "Bernard DeVoto and Kitty Smith," <u>New Republic</u> 144 (1937): 98.

SAMPLE BIBLIOGRAPHY PAGE

**Indent
second
line
5 spaces**

Bibliography   **Heading/Line 13**

Brooks, Wan Wyck. The Ordeal of Mark Twain. London: William   **First source/Line 17**
    Heinemann, 1922.

Canly, Henry Seidel. "Mark Twain Himself." Saturday Review of
    Literature, 9 (October 29, 1932), pp. 201-203.

Dell, Floyd. "Bernard DeVoto and Kitty Smity." New Republic, 144
    (January 23, 1937), pp. 98-99.

DeVoto, Bernard. Mark Twain's America. Cambridge, Mass.:
    Riverside Press, 1932.

Kaplan, Justin. Mr. Clemens and Mark Twain. New York: Simon and
    Schuster, 1966.

Leary, Lewis, ed. A Casebook on Mark Twain's Wound. New York:
    Thomas Y. Crowell, Co., 1962.

Lewis, Sinclair. "Fools, Liars, and Mr. DeVoto." Saturday Review
    of Literature, 27 (April 15, 1944), pp. 230-232.

Mattingly, Garrett. Bernard DeVoto: A Preliminary Appraisal.
    Boston: Little, Brown & Co., 1938.

Orlan, Sawey. Bernard DeVoto. New York: Twayne Publishers,
    1969.

VanDoren, Mark. "DeVoto's America." The Nation, 135 (October,
    1932), pp. 370-372.

APPENDIX H
Glossary of Research Terms
and Abbreviations

ABRIDGMENT—a shortened version of the author's original work.

ACKNOWLEDGE—to give credit to another person's words, ideas, or opinions in the form of a note and/or bibliography citation.

ALMANACS—published yearly, containing information and statistics on current events and some historical events.

ANNOTATED BIBLIOGRAPHY—a bibliography with critical and/or explanatory notes about each source.

ANALYSIS—a breaking up of a whole into its parts to examine them (often in a critical manner).

APPENDIX—a section containing material not included in the body but which is relevant to the topic. (Always titled with a letter as in Appendix A.)

ATLAS—a collection of maps. Some atlases also give historical changes and land-related statistics.

AUTHORITY—a generally accepted source of expert information.

AUTOBIOGRAPHY—a person's life story written by himself or herself.

BIBLIOGRAPHY (bib., bibliog.)—a list of books, articles, and other material used in a work or compiled about a topic.

BIOGRAPHY—a written account of a person's life.

BODY (of a paper)—refers to the paragraphs after the introduction and before the conclusion, contains the main points, ideas, and arguments of the author.

BRACKETS — the punctuation marks [   ] used only within a quoted passage to enclose additions (which explain a work or give information to the reader) in your own words. NOT the same as parentheses.

C or © — copyright, date of publication usually follows.

c. or ca. — circa — Latin, meaning "about." Used with approximate dates.

CALL NUMBER — the classification number of a book. (Located in upper left hand corner of the catalog and on the book's lower spine.)

CARD CATALOG — an alphabetical card file listing all books in the library, usually listed under author, title, and subject.

CITE, CITING, CITATION — to quote as an authority or example.

CLASSIFY, CLASSIFICATION — to arrange in classes or groups according to a system.

comp. — compiled by or compiler. A person who combines a work using several sources.

COMPARE, CONTRAST — to compare is to examine for similarities, to contrast is to examine for differences. Comparing and contrasting are often used together as a method of evaluation.

CROSS REFERENCE — words or symbols that refer the reader to other places where information may be found.

DESCRIPTORS — key words used in indexes. See KEY WORDS.

DOCUMENT — to acknowledge the source of an idea or fact with a footnote or endnote.

ed. or eds. — edited by or editor(s), one who prepares something for publication by selecting, revising, etc.

EDITION — the form in which a book is published.

EDITORIAL — an article expressing an opinion.

e.g. — for example, from the Latin *exempli gratia*. Used to indicate that an example follows.

ELLIPSIS — three periods with a space before, after, and between them (. . .) that indicate an omission in quoted material.

ENDNOTES — documentation located at the end of the paper.

et al. — and others, from the Latin *et alii*. Always abbreviate.

etc. — and so forth, from the Latin *et cetera*. Avoid use.

f. or ff. — following page or pages.

FOOTNOTE — (fn) used to describe citations at the bottom of a page. Use either footnotes or endnotes.

GENERAL ARTICLE — a relatively short article that gives a broad overview of a subject, usually located in encyclopedias, textbooks, etc.

GLOSSARY — a dictionary section, usually at the end of a book, in which technical or difficult words are explained.

ibid. — in the same place, from the Latin *ibidem*.

i.e. — that is, from the Latin *id est*.

INDEX — 1. A guide listed alphabetically with page numbers for locating all information in a book. 2. A reference work that gives the researcher the location of information on a topic.

KEY WORDS — terms related to your topic, usually naming important places, people, and subjects.

l. or ll., — line or lines.

LIBRARY CLASSIFICATION SYSTEMS — how books in the library are given call numbers. The two types of classification systems are Dewey Decimal and the Library of Congress.

MAGAZINE INDEX — microform index of more than 400 magazines.

MICROFORM — photographic reproductions of pages in printed matter, on acetate cards called microfiche or on rolls of 35mm film called microfilm.

MONOGRAPH — a written account of a single subject in one volume.

n.d. — no date of publication given.

n.p. — no publisher given, no place of publication.

ON LINE DATA BASE — computer access through telecommunications to holdings of other libraries (CARL), specialized indexes (SciSearch, Psychological Abstracts) and information services (UPI, Official Arlines Guide).

OUTLINE — a general plan of a work. There are several kinds of outlines: topic, sentence, phrase, word, preliminary. All outlines are used as organizational tools that encourage the writer to determine the main points of the presentation and the divisions under those points.

p. or pp. — page or pages. (*not* pg.)

PARAPHRASE — to put another's idea, opinion, or argument into your own words.

PARENTHESES — the punctuation marks ( ) used to enclose your own explanatory materials in a phrase or sentence of your own.

PERIODICALS — publications published at regular intervals — magazines, journals, etc.

PLAGIARISM — the stealing of another's style, ideas, or phrasing. To avoid plagiarism, everything not documented must consist of your ideas and word choices.

PRELIMINARY BIBLIOGRAPHY — see *working bibliography*. Bibliography cards containing the needed information about materials used in research. Used to see scope of sources and to help narrow the thesis.

PRELIMINARY OUTLINE — the initial outline constructed in order to direct the research.

PSEUDONYM — fictitious name used by an author.

PRIMARY SOURCE — the work, manuscript, journal, government document as originally written.

READERS' GUIDE — an index to the contents of 179 popular magazines.

REFERENCE book or REFERENCE — any source being read for information. Also may be a special section in the library where books such as almanacs, encyclopedias, and atlases are shelved.

ROUGH DRAFT — the first and any other writing before the paper is put into final form. Rough drafts often require several revisions.

ROMAN NUMERALS — numbering system used in outlines, for preliminary pages in books, sometimes used in volume numbers. (I-1, II-2, III-3, IV-4, V-5, VI-6, VII-7, VIII-8, IX-9, X-10, L-50, C-100)

SCAN — to make a quick reading of material in order to evaluate it.

SECONDARY SOURCE — a critical or historical work based on the primary source.

SEARS LIST OF SUBJECT HEADINGS — a source for alternative subject headings.

SERIES — thematically connected multivolume works.

SIRS — Social Issues Resource Series — group of indexed articles on social and scientific topics.

THESIS — the statement that explains the opinion or idea the writer wishes to support.

TITLE PAGE — the cover sheet for a research paper, which should include the title, author, course name, teacher, and the date.

tr., tran. — translator, translation, or translated by.

TRACINGS — subjects assigned to a book, listed at the bottom of the catalog card. Tracings suggest other subject headings to try.

vol., vols. — volume(s), numbers may be written in Arabic or Roman numerals.

WORKING BIBLIOGRAPHY — sometimes called a *preliminary bibliography*. A group of bibliography cards containing the needed information about materials used in research. Used to see scope of sources and to help narrow the thesis.

WORKING OUTLINE — the outline constructed in order to direct the research.

WORKS IN PROGRESS — works with a common index that are published at intervals.

ADDENDUM 1998

PROVIDED FOR UP-DATED
PURPOSES

BY

CRANBROOK KINGSWOOD
UPPER SCHOOL
LIBRARY DEPARTMENT

BASED ON:
MLA HANDBOOK FOR WRITERS OF
RESEARCH PAPERS,
4TH ED. NEW YORK:
MLA, 1995.

HOW TO CITE ELECTRONIC SOURCES

Listed below are examples of how to cite material from databases that are issued periodically. The style manual employed is: Gibaldi, Joseph. <u>MLA Handbook for Writers of Research Papers</u>. 4th ed. New York: MLA, 1995.

1. HOW TO CITE CRANBROOK'S NETWORK SOURCES

CITING <u>PROQUEST</u>

Access No:	02295068 ProQuest Periodical Abstracts
Title:	Columbia plugs in to Miles legacy
Authors:	Morris, Chris
Journal:	Billboard [GBIL] ISSN: 0006-2510 Jrnl Group: Business
	Vol: 107 Iss: 12 Date: Mar 25, 1995 p: 12, 91
	Type: Feature Length: Medium Illus: Photograph
Names:	Davis, Miles: Shorter, Wayne: Hancock, Herbie: Williams
	Tony: Roney, Wallace
Subjects:	Musical recordings; Jazz; Musicians & conductors; Musical performances

Abstract: On May 2, 1995, Columbia will release "The Complete Live At The Plugged Nickel 1965.: The eight-CD boxed set features two spectacular nights worth of performances by Miles Davis, Wayne Shorter, Herbie Hancock, Tony Williams and Wallace Roney at the Plugged Nickel, a now defunct club in Chicago. Item Availability: CD-ROM.

Bibliographic Citation:

Morris, Chris. "Columbia Plugs in to Miles Legacy" <u>Billboard</u> 25 Mar 1995: 12, 91 <u>General Periodicals Research I</u>. CD-ROM. UMI-Proquest. Aug. 1995

CITING <u>SIRS</u>

SIRS 1996 Consumerism. Electronic Only, Article 114

Subject	: Keyword (s) : Absolutely and Hodges	
Title	: You're Absolutely, Positively Pre-Approved. Maybe	
Author	: Glenn Hodges	
Source	: Washington Monthly	
Publication Date :	July/Aug. 1996	Page Number(s) : 42-45

WASHINGTON MONTHLY
July/Aug. 1996, pp. 42-45

"Reprinted with permission from THE WASHINGTON MONTHLY. Copyright by The Washington Monthly Company, 1611 Connecticut Avenue, NW, Washington, D.C. 20009. (202) 462-0128 "

YOU'RE ABSOLUTELY, POSITIVELY PRE-APPROVED. MAYBE
by Glenn Hodges

How Credit Card Companies Twist the Truth--And Why Regulators Let Them.

G \citing.doc

Bibliographic Citation:

Hodges, Glenn. "You're Absolutely, Positively Pre-Approved. Maybe."
    Washington Monthly, July/Aug. 1996: 42-45. SIRS Consumerism 1996. Art. 114.
    SIRS Researcher CD-ROM. CD-ROM. SIRS. Winter 1996.

2. HOW TO CITE CD-ROM SOURCES

If no printed source or printed analogue is indicated for the material you are citing, your entry in the works-cited list should consist of the following items: Name of the author, title of the material accessed (in quotation marks), date of the material (if given), title of the database including the version number (underlined), publication medium (CD-ROM), name of the vendor (if relevant), electronic publication date.

David Garrows "King, Martin Luther, Jr." The World Book Multimedia Encyclopedia, Version 3.2.
    CD-ROM. World Book, Inc., 1996.

3. HOW TO CITE INTERNET SOURCES
(Using various access methods shouldn't substantively change citation style)
Listed below are examples taken from the MLA Handbook for Writers of Research Papers. 4th ed.
New York: MLA, 1995

E-MAIL, LISTSERV, AND NEWSLIST CITATIONS
Give the author's name (if known), the subject line from the posting in quotation marks, and the address of the listserv or newslist, along with the date. For personal e-mail listings, the address may be omitted.

Lovett, Richard. "Discussion of Teacher Traits." Psycholquy (June 1996) E-mail.
    psych@ducc Message: Get psyc 93-xxxx.

Seabrook Richard H. C. "Community and Progress." cybermind@jefferson.village.
    virginia.edu (22 Jan. 1997).

Thomson, Barry. "Virtual Reality." Personal e-mail (25 Jan. 1997)

FILE TRANSFER PROTOCOL - FTP
To cite files available for downloading via ftp, give the author's name (if known), the full title of the paper in quotation marks, and the address of the ftp site along with the full path to follow to find the paper, and the date of access.

Rabine, Richard. "Preservation in Driving Habits." Psycholoquy
    FTP: Hostname duke.eduDirectory:pub/harnad/Psycholoquy/1993.Volume 4 File
    psycoloquy.93.4.13.base-rate.12.rabine (June 1996)

GOPHER Sites
(Information available via gopher search protocols)

For information found using gopher search protocols, list the author's name, the title of the paper in quotation marks, any print publication information, and the gopher search path followed to access the information, including the date that the file was accessed.

Quittner, Joshua. "Far Out: Welcome to Their World Built of MUD." Published in *Newsday*, 7 Nov. 1993. gopher/University of Koeln/About MUDs, MOOs and MUSEs in Education/Selected Papers/newsday (5 Dec 1996).

TELNET SITES
(Sites and Files available via the telnet protocol)

List the author's name (if known), the title of the work (if shown) in quotation marks, the title of the full work if applicable in italics, and the complete telnet address, along with directions to access the publication, along with the date of visit.

Gornes, Lee. "Xerox's On-Line Neighborhood: A Great Place to Visit." *Mercury News* 3 May 1992. telnet lambda.parc.xerox.com 8888,@go #50827, press 13 (5 Dec 1996).

WWW Sites (World Wide Web)
(Available via Lynx, Netscape, Other Web Browsers)

To cite files available for viewing/downloading via the World Wide Web, give the author's name (if known), the full title of the work in quotation marks, the title of the complete work if applicable in italics, the last date the site was updated or revised (if known), the full http address, and the date of visit.

Burka, Lauren P. "A Hypertext History of Multi-User Dimensions." *MUD History* http://www.ccs.neu.edu/home/lpb/mud-history.html (5 Dec. 1996).

ASSESSING A WEB SITE

How to determine whether the information you've found is fact or fiction.

Search terms (keywords, subject headings) used:
Search engine used:

Criteria for determining worth of a web site:

1. Authority
   Who is sponsoring the Page? Name and address of author(s)
   Web site address:

2. Accuracy
   Are the souces used in creating the site clearly cited?
   What are they?

3. Objectivity
   Is the site a public service/free of advertising?

4. Currency
   When was the site last up-dated?

5. Coverage
   Is the page completed or in progress?

6. Domain Name
   Does the domain name (or the last three letters of the address) match the
      type of individual or groups represented?
      Examples:
      .com = commercial
      .gov = governmental
      .edu = educational institutions
      .mil = military
      .org = other organizations
      .net = network resourses

HOW TO CITE INTERNET SOURCES

*Listed below is an example taken from the <u>MLA Handbook for Writers of Research Papers</u>.
4th ed. New York: MLA, 1995.*

WWW Sites (World Wide Web)

   To cite files available for viewing/downloading via the World Wide Web, give the author's
name (if known), the full title of the work in quotation marks, the title of the complete work if
applicable in italics, the last date the site was updated or revised (if known), the full http address, and the
date of visit.

Burka, Lauren P. "A Hypertext History of Multi-User Dimensions." *MUD History*.
      http://www.ccs.neu.edu/home/lpb/mud-history.html (5 Dec. 1996).